THE PORCUPINE BOOK OF VERSE

THE PORCUPINE BOOK OF VERSE

art by Don Robison

CONCORDIA
Publishing House
St. Louis   London

Concordia Publishing House, St. Louis, Missouri
Concordia Publishing House Ltd., London, E. C. 1
Copyright © 1974 by Concordia Publishing House
ISBN 0-570-06995-5

Manufactured in the United States of America

CONTENTS

POEMS ABOUT PEOPLE

POEMS ABOUT ANIMALS

POEMS ABOUT THINGS

POEMS ABOUT NATURE

POEMS ABOUT NIGHT AND DAY

POEMS ABOUT PEOPLE

WHAT HAPPENED TO ALICE

1 *One is Alice all alone.*

2 *Two is sly Fox on the phone.*

3 *Three is hungry Crocodile.*

4 *Four is Lion's greedy smile.*

Five is Hippopotamus, empty top to bottomus.

Six is Grizzly, large and cavernous.

Seven is Tiger, always ravenous.

Eight is when they sneaked about.

Nine is when they all jumped out!

Ten is Alice's birthday party.
They all had lots to eat.

7   **—Joan Chase Bacon**

THE FOOLISH GARDENER

There was a certain gardener
Who made a grave mistake,
A worse mistake I dare to say
Than anyone should make.

He planted his potato patch
Too near his onion bed,
Which isn't very wise at all,
As I have often said.

The potatoes grew quite weepy
And mad as anything;
Their eyes got full of onion juice,
Which made them smart and sting.

Their eyes became all clouded up,
Which isn't good, you know,
Because in that condition
They couldn't see to grow.

—*Eupha Whitworth Richie*

8

MARSHA COFFY

Marsha Coffy and I took a tin can full of rocks
next door to give to Mrs. Gibbs
and she liked them very much
and kept one as a present from me
and another as a present from Marsha
and put them in the bottom of a pot
to help a flower catch its breath.

—Antonio L. Betancourt

JAMIE, SUSIE, AND SAM

Oh, what a day to be at the beach
and dig in the sand for a clam,
watching whitecaps ride the crest of a wave
with Jamie,
          Susie,
                    and Sam!

They live on the shore and I visit,
a most fortunate person I am,
being invited to share in the fun
with Jamie,
          Susie,
                    and Sam!

10

The castles we build are tremendous!
   We form private lakes with a dam.
   I am one of the crew on the king's pleasure boats
   with Jamie,
            Susie,
                and Sam!

We climbed to the top of a lighthouse,
   walked seawalls, found treasures, and swam.
   Oh, what a day it has been at the beach
   with Jamie,
            Susie,
                and Sam!

—Frances Wiegand

11

POEMS ABOUT ANIMALS

THE OCTOPUS

The octopus is a strange sort of creature,
With tentacles his mostly feature.

He lives in the depths of the saltwater ocean
And changes color to suit his notion.

In climbing things he takes no risks,
For he's equipped with suction disks.

And he swims by means of a high-powered jet,
So transportation's an easy bet.

When something comes along twice his size,
He just squirts ink in the monster's eyes.

All this is handy, I must agree,
But still I'm glad that he isn't me,

For I shouldn't like to have it said
That I had my feet growing out of my head.

—Eupha Whitworth Richie

THE LUCKY ELEPHANT

The elephant has lots of luck
 And pleasure, it appears,
For when he's hot, he fans himself
 With his enormous ears.
He likes his peanuts and his hay
 At almost any hour,
And takes up water in his trunk
 To give himself a shower.
And when at last he's cool and clean,
 With happiness aglow,
He plays upon his trumpet then
 So everyone will know!

—*Anne Jennings*

THE FIREFLY

Anton Cooper gave me a bottle
with a little firefly in it
that blinked his light
and winked at me
off and on . . .
on and off . . .
as it walked around
the bottom of the jar;
and I thanked Anton Cooper
very much;
then I waited a while,
for one more blink,
and then I let it go.

—*Antonio L. Betancourt*

15

POUNDS AND POUNDS
OF HUNTING HOUNDS

Pounds and pounds of hunting hounds
from midnight until noon,
chased through the woods
and never found the smart raccoon.

Baying, barking ceaselessly,
jumping brush and logs,
running in mad circles,
those pounds of hunting dogs.

The raccoon watched them from a tree
and, funny as it sounds,
enjoyed the mass confusion
of the pounds of hunting hounds!

—Frances Wiegand

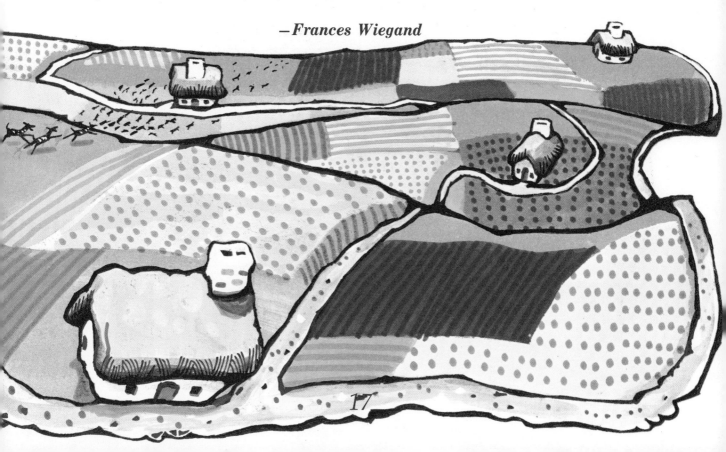

17

ALPHABET SOUP

I always have fun with my alphabet soup—
I play every letter's a fish.
The g is a goldfish, the b is a bass,
Both hidden deep down in my dish.
The p stands for pike, and the c for a cod;
The e that's an eel is quite tame.
The t is a trout; there are lots and lots more,
But truly too many to name.
My alphabet-fish have the funniest shapes,
Some thin and some round as a moon.
At last, when I'm tired of playing pretend,
I catch them, each one, with my spoon!

—Anne Jennings

THE BUTTON

Today I found a button
that was very shiny
and white,
and it had four holes
where you put the thread,
and it looked just like
the buttons on my shirt,
only different,
and I am going to keep it
in the top drawer
of my dresser
forever;
but I must not put it
in my mouth.

—*Antonio L. Betancourt*

BUBBLE GUM TREE

If bubble gum grew on a tree,
How utterly grand that would be!
When the wind came along,
It would blow and blow,
And all of the bubbles
Would start to grow,
As big as balls,
As big as balloons,
And maybe as big
As big round moons,
On that very elastic
And simply fantastic
Bubble gum tree.

—Eupha Whitworth Richie

21

INSIDE/OUTSIDE

I put my foot
inside my shoe,
my coat's for
outside wear,

and when I eat,
the food goes in—
it does the most good there!

22

When I play,
it's out of doors,
my friends live all
over town,

and when I sleep,
I snuggle warm
inside my
eiderdown.

—Candyce Clayton

UPSIDE / DOWNSIDE

Salt pours from a shaker bottle
upside down.
Steam floats from a singing kettle
ceiling bound.

Sun shoots down from the
high up sky,
like rain and sleet and snow,
but the green green plants
start as seeds in the ground,
and it's up straight up
that they grow.

—Candyce Clayton

THE OVEN

He's truly very kind and good
 And friendly as can be,
Receiving dishes of all sorts,
 So cold and shivery.
Then patiently he heats and bakes
The roasts and casseroles and cakes.
When faithfully he's warmed them through
 As well as he is able,
He lets them out, all piping hot,
 And sends them to the table.

—Anne Jennings

THE SANDBOX

I always keep a silver shovel
in the sandbox,
and a few blocks of wood
for bridges,
and a stick or two for trees,
when I make a house,
and a red plastic bucket
with a lot of water in it;
and when it is hot,
I dig away
the sand on top
and sit where it is cool.

—Antonio L. Betancourt

POTATO EYES

The little potato said,
   "How I despise
   the need to have glasses
   for all of my eyes!

"But, my doctor told me
   that he would advise
   lenses and frames
   to be fitted to size,

"Different prescriptions,
    bifocals and tris,
  some tinted, depending
    on tests, I surmise.

"To be set for the day,
    do you realize,
  for proper adjustment
    I'll start at sunrise?

"I'd almost rather
    be cut into fries
  than wipe each lens gently
    should I get the cries.

"I have faith in my doctor
    and know he is wise.
  If my vision improves,
    what a pleasant surprise!"

—Frances Wiegand

29

POEMS ABOUT NATURE

GRASSY LAWN

By day her blades are banners fine,
Each waving at the sky;
At night she is a friendly bed,
Where sleeping moonbeams lie.

—Anne Jennings

THE MAGIC POPPER

June shakes her magic popper now,
Down low and way up high;
And giant puffs of popcorn clouds
Explode against the sky.

—Anne Jennings

SPRING PRAYER

When sweet blue eyes of violets
Are shining from the grass,
And little breezes touch the leaves
So gently as they pass,
When daisies nod their petaled heads,
And happy robins sing,
I thank You, Father, from my heart,
Because You've sent the spring.

—Anne Jennings

SUMMER PRAYER

I love the summer's voices, God:
The laughter of the breeze,
The whisper of the raindrops too,
The singing of the trees,
The rustle of the bushes green,
The calling of a bird.
My thanks for summer's voices, God,
The sweetest I have heard.

—Anne Jennings

FALL PRAYER

This fall each little maple tree
Is wearing autumn finery,
A gay bright smoke of red and gold,
All fringed in sunbeams, warm and bold.
The river, as it flows along,
Will murmur its contented song.
The mums wear paint-box colors all.
. . . I thank You, Father, for the fall.

—Anne Jennings

WINTER PRAYER

I thank You, God, for winter time,
    When loud and playful north winds blow,
When all the bushes and the trees
    Wear their white woolly gloves of snow.

The little brook is quiet now
    Below his shining icy sheath;
I listen and can almost hear
    The frozen music underneath.

Sometimes my friends will skate with me.
    We jump in drifts of snow together;
And I repeat my little prayer:
    I thank You, God, for winter weather.

—Anne Jennings

A PUZZLE

Why do the trees take off their clothes
When cold winds start to blow?
It seems such folly to undress
When almost time for snow.

Then they should keep their leafy robes,
Or so it seems to me.
I would be cold with long bare limbs,
But then, I'm not a tree.

—Eupha Whitworth Richie

POEMS ABOUT NIGHT AND DAY

NIGHT

Bugs creep,
rabbits leap,
crickets cheep,
stars peep,
I sleep.

—Virginia Mueller

41

NIGHT THINGS

With the night in my eyes
there's nothing I can see
except all the funny animals
hiding from me.

There are elephants from Africa
in the cupboards, I'm sure,
and a Tasmanian monster
behind the front door.

I've a panther in the coalbin
and a whale in the garage,
but my parents never see them;
they think it's a mirage!

—Candyce Clayton

DAY THINGS

With the day in my eyes
I can see far and wide;
my invisible friend
never strays from my side.

The two of us roam
in clever disguise
and track down things
you can't see with your eyes,

like high flying oophals
and low crawling smooj
and by the end of the day
we're too tracked out to move!

—Candyce Clayton

45

NIGHT PRAYER

I love to look outside at night,
    At moonlight in bright bars
And soft dark skies, all covered with
    Wide curtains hung with stars.

The blinking stars are gentle eyes.
    In quiet, cool and deep,
They watch me in my little bed
    While I am fast asleep.

Dear God, who made the smiling moon
    And star-eyes, silver-white,
I thank You for Your care of me
    All through the velvet night.

—Anne Jennings

DAY PRAYER

This morning, shortly after dawn,
The sunlight lay upon the lawn
Like little saucers, glowing bright,
That spilled a foam of golden light.
. . . Dear God, the day has just begun.
I thank You for the morning sun.

—Anne Jennings